STEAM MEMORIES: 1950'

No.12: DEVON & CORNWALL LINES

Great Western & Southern Region
Including Locomotive Depots & Branch Lines

BOOK LAW PUBLICATIONS

Copyright Book Law Publications 2008
ISBN 978-1901-945-638

INTRODUCTION

In 1956, and again in 1960, railway photographer Don Beecroft took holidays in Devon and Cornwall during which he travelled widely throughout both counties. Most of the travelling was done by rail and so he was constrained slightly by the timetables and availability of certain services. However, during the periods he was waiting for connections he took advantage of what was there to photograph and it is from his unique collection that we have put together this album of the railway scene which he witnessed.

The 1956 holiday was taken during July whilst the 1960 fortnight overlapped the end of August and beginning of September. Both periods captured the summer timetable movements which, in some areas, brought a steady stream of photogenic subjects. In other places the lengthy periods of quiet were broken by short bursts of intense activity when it was impossible to be in two places at the same time and so 'brilliant opportunities' were sometimes missed.

We have not followed rigidly in Don's footsteps and have instead taken an imaginary journey from the eastern border of south Devon, along its southern coast, into Cornwall via the Western Region main line and down to Penzance. Then we doubled back, taking in eastern Cornwall and capturing the former London & South Western Railway delights of the North Cornwall line and the outposts in Devon. During our journey we have used an imaginary time machine to flit from one period to another and then back again - very useful indeed.

It has been immensely enjoyable putting the album together. It brought back many happy memories for us and we hope that you too will get as much out of it as we have.

David Allen, Newstead Abbey, 2008.

(*previous page*) **Bodmin Road station - a scruffy Collett 'Hall', No.4924 EYDON HALL, departs with a Plymouth to Penzance local in July 1956.**

Printed and bound by The Amadeus Press, Cleckheaton, West Yorkshire.
First published in the United Kingdom by Book Law Publications, 382 Carlton Hill, Nottingham, NG4 1JA

Axminster was the first station in Devon when travelling from London over the former London & South Western main line from Salisbury. It was here in August 1903 that a junction was created with a branch for Lyme Regis leading off the main line to Exeter. It was no simple junction either. From the start the traffic Department did not want the branch trains conflicting with the main line at Axminster and so they built a flyover which carried the branch from the terminal platform, hidden behind the locomotive, across from the Up side platform. The branch then ran away from the main line for about 250 yards before turning towards the south and west for another 250 yards during which time it had risen sufficiently to bridge, or flyover, the main line. It then turned due south and headed off to Lyme Regis. There was also a direct connection from the Down side to the branch which was situated just behind the photographer. The train is a Waterloo to Plymouth express and it is September 1960. There was still lots of interest in taking holidays in Devon and Cornwall and the railways catered for much of the traffic from far-off towns and cities. 'Battle of Britain' No.34064 FIGHTER COMMAND is not looking its best here but it had recently been 'in shops' for a Light Intermediate overhaul when AWS and a speedometer were fitted. at this time it was allocated to Exmouth Junction engine shed and was into its second year at that establishment. No doubt the Pacific will work this train through to Plymouth and retire to Friary shed for servicing. Prior to the opening of the branch to Lyme Regis, Axminster could boast to having a one road engine shed which was situated just to the right of where the stationary brakevan is stabled.

Working hard up the 1 in 80 gradient towards the flyover, 416 class Atlantic tanks Nos.30583 and 30582 lift a heavy Lyme Regis bound holiday train out of Axminster in early September 1960. From this spot the train will curve round behind the photographer before crossing the bridge over the main line. The short section of level track on either side of the flyover was the only respite these engines would get for the next three miles of the mainly 1 in 40 climb up to virtually 500ft near Shapwick hill. Another short climb would bring them to the only intermediate station on the branch at Combpyne which opened with the branch and also closed with it. After that it was virtually down hill all the way to Lyme Regis and the terminus. For the return journey back to Axminster the engines faced another formidable climb out of the seaside resort back up to Combpyne station. Two of the three Adams designed 4-4-2 tank engines which worked this branch in British Railways days had been active on the line for much of its existence (the third engine was No.30584 and was the first of the trio to be withdrawn) and they worked one engine on the branch with two at Exmouth Junction shed either working locally or in repair. During the summer holiday periods it was quite usual to have two engines on the branch, as here, with the third in reserve. The 4-4-2Ts first came to the Lyme branch in 1913 and had replaced the resident O2 class 0-4-4Ts which were not suited to the branch because of its extremely harsh curvature. A small shed, with adjacent coal stage, was established for one engine at Lyme Regis when the branch was opened but ten years later the shed was burnt down. A new steel framed shed was quickly provided and sufficed to closure of the branch on 29th November 1965. By then of course the Adams tank had long been superseded by Ivatt LMS designed Class 2 2-6-2T. The attractive LSWR engines had been taken off the branch in July 1961 and sent for scrapping but one of them was picked out for preservation.

Our next stop is at Seaton Junction, long remembered by this writer for its inclusion, as an article, on the BBC television programme *Railway Roundabout* during the late fifties, or was it the early sixties? This was yet another main line station catering for a small yet once popular seaside resort some four miles away to the south. In this September 1960 view of the junction station we see N15 'King Arthur' No.30796 SIR DODINAS LE SAVAGE at the head of a short morning Exeter to Salisbury stopping train. The Maunsell 4-6-0 was allocated to Salisbury shed at this time and had been since May 1959. It was destined to end its working days there and was condemned at Eastleigh works in February 1962. Most of the West of England expresses sped through here over the fast lines, shaking the station as they did, but certain seasonal workings from London stopped to unload holidaymakers for Seaton. The whole station was completely remodelled and widened during 1927-28, the Southern Railway at that time was a great believer in concrete, hence the platforms and footbridges are constructed of that material. The LSWR designed station house, which dated from the 1860's, was retained and can be seen behind the locomotive. Another relic of the past stands in a slightly elevated position just north of the station - the Shute Arms Hotel - the ideal hostelry for train watchers of the time. We have no photographs of London trains either speeding through or stopping so we go to our next picture of the branch goods engine - M7 No.30045.

M7 No.30045 has just worked in from Exmouth Junction shed and is here to work the goods traffic onto and off the Seaton branch. Passing through the station on the Up side, the 0-4-4T will proceed eastwards to the end of the four track section in order to set back onto the Down main line, through the station in a westerly direction to the junction with the Seaton branch. The branch line was opened in 1868 by the Seaton & Beer Railway and, by Agreement, it was worked by the L&SWR from the start, a wooden shed being provided for the branch engine at Seaton terminus. Over the years the shed deteriorated so in 1937 the Southern built a new one on a different site out of the 'in vogue' concrete blocks. Seaton station had been rebuilt at the same time in the SR art deco concrete style. The branch engine lived here all week and only went to Exmouth Junction shed at weekends for the necessary servicing and maintenance. No.30045 might even have been changing over with the branch engine so that it then became the branch engine for the week but more than likely it was here to collect and distribute the goods. When the Western Region took over this section of the old LSWR in 1963, they wasted no time at all in getting rid of the M7 class engines in favour of their Pannier tanks - Nos.6400, 6412 and 6430 were sent in March to work from Exmouth Junction depot. But worse was to come later in the year when two-car diesel units were introduced onto the branch and the little engine shed at Seaton was closed during November. In August 1964 it was possible to see ex Southern locomotives working the branch again but these comprised the 2-6-0 tender engines of the U class. The inevitable took place in March 1966 when the whole branch, from the junction to Seaton and including the two intermediate stations at Colyton and Colyford, and Seaton Junction was closed. Note the number of passengers on platform No.1, waiting no doubt for the next London bound train. Behind the station building was a large rail served Express Dairies milk depot, the roofs of certain buildings therein being visible in this view. From this place, and like many similar plants dotted around the West Country, vast quantities of milk was despatched daily in rail tankers to London and its suburbs - that traffic has now been lost to road transport. Working the Seaton branch must have been a good omen for the 64XX Pannier tanks - two of the three have been preserved.

Continuing west along the exLSWR main line, we do not travel too far before we come across a further junction station - Sidmouth Junction. This place was yet another inland station (160 miles from Waterloo) sat in the middle of nowhere, with very little population, and which had the sole purpose of serving the branch trains to Sidmouth and Exmouth on the coast. In September 1960 we see one of Exmouth Junction's unrebuilt 'West Country' Pacifics No.34096 TREVONE starting off from the Down platform at Sidmouth Junction in order to gain the Up main. The train was bound for Waterloo and had started out as two separate portions, one from Exmouth and the other from Sidmouth which had been joined together at Tipton St Johns, then worked off the branch and directly into the Down platform at Sidmouth Junction by a couple of Standard tanks. The Pacific had then backed onto the train ready for the off. Opened in July 1860, this station was originally called Feniton after the nearby settlement directly east of the station. However, during the following year it was renamed Ottery Road, probably on account that said road crossed over the main line at the western end of the station. In 1874

We have already seen N15 No.30796 at Seaton Junction but here at Sidmouth Junction on the following day, in early September 1960, it is on the same duty with the same carriage set plying between Exeter and Salisbury. As can be seen, the level crossing at Ottery Road is still in operation, even the busy summer season rail traffic is not inconveniencing the locals too much. The delicate looking signal post, with the lofty repeater signal, shows that a Down working is imminent. The reopening of the station here in 1971 was brought about by the then recent and growing residential development in the area, this mass of housing now centres more on the railway station than on the original village to the east.

Our next stop is Exmouth Junction engine shed where, on the south side of the shed building, we find unrebuilt 'West Country' No.34011 TAVISTOCK being prepared, in September 1960, for a westbound working from Exeter (St Davids). This was a 72A engine at this time, having transferred from Nine Elms in March 1959. Never rebuilt, this Pacific was one of the early withdrawals, succumbing in November 1963 and being cut up at Eastleigh works, a fate most of the class escaped. The tender coupled to No.34011 was acquired in June 1947 (No.3263), it second and last since building. Note the tender has cut down sides, an alteration carried out during a 'General' in the summer of 1952. During another overhaul, a Light Intermediate performed at Eastleigh in March 1960, the engine was fitted with a speedometer and AWS, the battery for the latter device, immediately below the feet of one of the depot's 'disposal gang', defacing the front end. The smoke deflector still carries the bracket for fixing the *DEVON BELLE* wingplates, long after this locomotive had left the county in April 1951 on transfer to London.

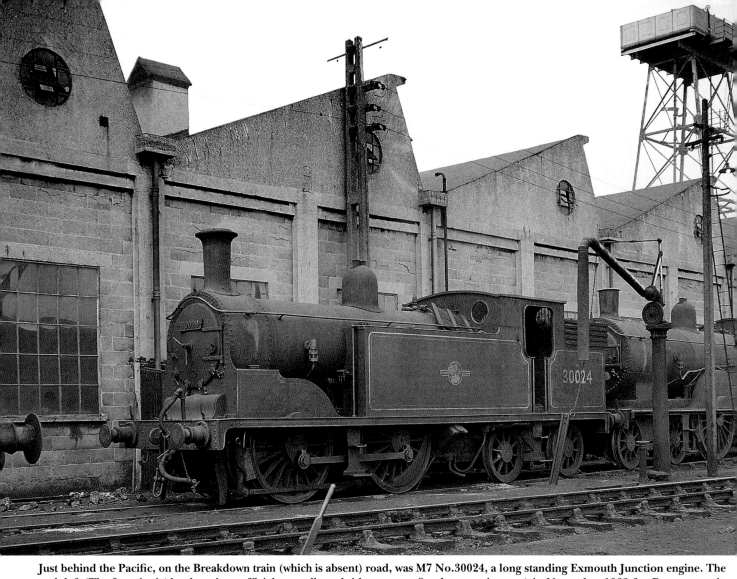

Just behind the Pacific, on the Breakdown train (which is absent) road, was M7 No.30024, a long standing Exmouth Junction engine. The tank left 'The Junction' (the depot's unofficial yet well used title amongst Southern enginemen) in November 1962 for Bournemouth, and an uncertain future which took it into Eastleigh works during the following March, never to come out again. This engine had been constructed at Nine Elms works in January 1899 when the L&SWR still had its locomotive headquarters in London. The original class of 105 engines was virtually intact when British Railways took them over; only one had been scrapped back in 1937. Another was lost to a bizarre accident in May 1948 but withdrawals proper did not begin until 1957, a time when most of the class were either sixty years of age or fast approaching that milestone; many actually passed it, which was attributed to the designer Dugald Drummond. The proximity of the 0-4-4T to the shed wall enables us to see the architecture and materials involved in the construction of this shed during the long and protracted rebuilding throughout most of the twenties. Once again we can see the chosen medium is concrete, the nearby Southern Railway concrete plant supplying the pre-cast panels, window lintels, and screen blocks. Brought under the Western Region umbrella in September 1963, the depot closed in March 1967 but not before it had changed code from 72A to 83D (Plymouth Laira's old code) and had banished steam in June 1965.

The turntable at Exmouth Junction engine shed was situated in the south-east corner of the depot, alongside the main line. One day in early September 1960 'Merchant Navy' No.35007 ABERDEEN COMMONWEALTH was ready to be turned for the next working home to Salisbury. This Pacific had been rebuilt in May 1958, virtually sixteen years and nearly 800,000 miles after entering traffic at Salisbury in June 1942. In this rebuilt condition the locomotive was to run a further half million miles in revenue earning service prior to withdrawal in July 1967. By then it was allocated to Nine Elms shed having transferred from Weymouth in April 1967; Salisbury had reluctantly given it up in January 1965, not too long after it had completed a Heavy Intermediate overhaul when it was in 'good nick'. The 70ft diameter articulated turntable was fairly young compared to the rebuilt depot and was only installed in March 1947, replacing a 65ft electrically operated, balanced table which dated from about the early days of the Great War and was obviously worn out.

This is what it looked like before the NRM got hold of it and sectioned it in 1974. No.35029 ELLERMAN LINES, rebuilt during the summer of 1959, and seen at Exmouth Junction shed a year later in September 1960. The Nine Elms allocated engine is turned, prepared and ready to work back home to Waterloo. With another six years of work still in front of it, the 'Merchant Navy' would ply the route between London and Exeter many more times during that period and, after moving to Weymouth in September 1964, it worked the route through Bournemouth for the last two years before withdrawal. Considering it then spent nearly seven years in open storage at Barry, the 'guts' of the engine were in a remarkable condition when it was 'opened up'.

To gain access to the former Great Western main line we have now travelled down to Exeter (St Davids), by-passing Central station (photographically) but still with the Southern in the form of unrebuilt 'West Country' No.34024 TAMAR VALLEY which has charge of a four vehicle Waterloo-Ilfracombe train in September 1960. Besides this duty, the external condition of the Pacific gives a clue as to its home shed - Exmouth Junction - which employed, before World War Two, more than eighty cleaners. Times certainly were changing in the sixties, just as they did during the previous decade. Salvation for this engine was just months away because in December it entered Eastleigh for rebuilding and would emerge in mid February with a sparkling coat of paint covering new bodywork and looking a completely different locomotive. In November 1963 No.34024 transferred to Bournemouth where the cleaning regime was a little better but we were now in the age of the diesel and everything clean and new was being lavished on the new motive power - steam was the unwanted, unclean and unkempt. TAMAR VALLEY was withdrawn in July 1967, one of the last steam locomotives to go on the Southern, of course by then its nameplates had been removed and its numbers virtually non-existent beneath a thick covering of grime. St Davids station in the meantime would carry on, regardless of what hauled the trains in or out. Note that the SR train is waiting at the centre island platform - Nos.3 and 4 - which had been used by the L&SWR, the Southern and later the SR since the station had undergone reconstruction in the three years preceding the Great War. The L&SWR did not reach this station until 1862, some eighteen years after the Bristol & Exeter Railway had created the first station on the site. In the intervening years further companies arrived at St Davids and a vast increase in traffic forced a large reconstruction to be carried out just as the L&SW came down the incline from their station at Queen Street (later Central). So, various agreements between the Great Western and the London & South Western culminated in the traffic patterns we observe here with trains from London arriving at both ends of the station and the Southern Region traffic having exclusive use of platforms 3 and 4 and the Western Region using all the other platforms. Of course, the exclusivity was not held to the letter and whenever traffic demands deemed a change of platform usage it took place. Note the Z class tank No.30955 on the through road waiting for its next banking job up to Central station.

Our introduction to the Western Region at Exeter (St Davids) brings us to the north end of platform No.5 where Exeter's own 'Castle' No.5075 WELLINGTON heads the Up *ROYAL DUCHY* in September 1960. Looking somewhat scruffy, the 4-6-0 has just taken this train over from a couple of smaller 4-6-0s which had brought the afternoon Paddington bound express in from Cornwall. From here we will head in the opposite direction to this train, retracing its steps, so to speak, into Cornwall along the Great Western main line via Newton Abbot and Plymouth.

Exeter (St Davids) station, Tuesday 30th August 1960. Just before we board our train, the afternoon Taunton-Newton Abbot local, there is time to take this picture of it standing at platform No.1 with Collett 'Hall' No.5976 ASHWICKE HALL at the head. Up until January 1959 this 4-6-0 had been based at Exeter shed but it was then transferred to Old Oak Common, however, on this August day in 1960 it is not only working a local turn, it was also still wearing an 83C (Exeter St Davids) shed plate. So, did the transfer ever take place or had it returned to Exeter shed during the interim period without 'official' notice being published? Its external condition would suggest that it was definately an 83C engine. The first floor of the main building at St Davids station always appeared to have an unfinished look about it, perhaps earlier plans suggested an overall roof or some other grandiose scheme which never materialised. 15

Winding our way now along the WR main line towards Plymouth, with a few deviations on the way, we next come to Newton Abbot where, in July 1956 - yes we have gone back in time - a locomotive works, engine shed and junction station employed a large proportion of the town's population. From this place branch lines left the main line to reach into the heart of the south Devon countryside at Moretonhampstead and Christow (this latter village once connected directly to Exeter via a twisting yet picturesque single line route which left the main line at Alphington), two places still doing business but only just because they were soon to lose their passenger services - 2nd march 1959 and 9th June 1958 respectively - total closure of course would not be far behind. Moretonhampstead could at one time boast a single road engine shed which although closed in November 1947, was still standing and in private use up to at least 1995. After the branch locomotive vacated the substantial 1866 stone-built edifice on the eve of Nationalisation, it was used by the local coal merchant to store coal until BR sold the site; the generous doorway was built to broad gauge standard. Anyway, here we are at Newton Abbot where trains for Torbay would call before they left the main line at Aller junction and followed the branch to Kingswear. A lot of engine changing took place at Newton Abbot and heavy westbound trains (they nearly all were post-war) stopped to take on a pilot engine to help out over the south Devon banks encountered before Plymouth. This train appears to be a semi-fast which is probably on its way to Bristol, the 'County' in charge No.1000 COUNTY OF MIDDLESEX being a Bath Road engine at that time. It has possibly just worked off the Kingswear branch calling at Paignton and Torquay en route. Next stop Teignmouth then Dawlish, Exeter.....magic stuff. This 4-6-0 had spent two years (1951 and 52) allocated to Laira shed where its high boiler pressure combined with its 6ft 3in. coupled wheels made it ideal for working the main line through Cornwall besides the formidable south Devon banks. Penzance and Truro also had a couple each for much of the BR period so that a third of the class was allocated to West Country depots at any one time.

Resting on shed at Newton Abbot, on Thursday 8th September 1960, is 'King' No.6002 KING WILLIAM IV of Plymouth Laira shed. The premier GWR motive power for many years, this class of locomotive had reigned supreme on the heavy West of England expresses to and from Paddington. Even up to the end of 1957 there had been nine of the class permanently allocated to Laira depot. However, in the late summer of 1960 that number was down to just two (No.6016 was the other one) and No.6002 here was only allocated for a fifteen month spell away from Old Oak Common - by the middle of September 1960 (just five days after this picture was captured) both 'Kings' would have left Plymouth for London and Laira depot would never again have them 'on the books'. A long-time resident of Laira, this engine started its career there in July 1927 just thirteen days after the first of the class was put into traffic. Virtually the whole of the Great Western era was spent working from Plymouth with short, occasional, loans to Newton Abbot or Exeter St Davids sheds. Considering the engine had not been in works since early summer of 1959, the external condition is indeed commendable, Laira shed still regarding them as worthy of a clean and polish. Like many of its class, this engine ended up working out its last few years of operation from Stafford Road shed in Wolverhampton where in September 1962 the remaining resident 'Kings' were withdrawn en masse. No.6002 was sold for scrap in February 1963 and on the day it was hauled away to Cox & Danks it was covered in frost.

Still at Newton Abbot on Thursday 8th September 1960, we meet 'Grange' No.6845 PAVILAND GRANGE which has just pulled up at platform No.5 with a six-coach Plymouth-Bristol stopping train. The 5ft 8in. coupled wheels of this class of locomotive were ideal for this type of start-stop working, where acceleration from the numerous station stops was easily gained and then a decent running speed was maintained prior to the next stop. No.6845 was another Laira based engine and possibly it could have been working this turn whilst it was on its way to a new home at Oxley depot in Wolverhampton because it was transferred to 84B in September 1960. Prior to June, this 4-6-0 was based at Penzance (they were well-liked at 83G and preferable over the 'Hall' class) but was then transferred to Laira, the first step in its northward shift from Cornwall to the West Midlands. Withdrawn at Tyseley shed in September 1964 (it is amazing how many events on the railway took place in September), the 'Grange' was sold for scrap to Cashmores and entered their Great Bridge yard in December 1964.

Leaving the main line for a while at Aller junction, we now head due south towards Kingswear on the branch to Torbay. Our first encounter, in the deteriorating weather, is this '5101' class 2-6-2T accelerating out of Torquay, en route to Kingswear, No.4150 is just about to dive beneath the beautiful iron bridge spanning the line at the south end of the station. This does not appear to be a local working, although the motive power seems to contradict that thought. It was most probably a portion detached from a Cornwall or Plymouth bound express at Newton Abbot. The large 'Prairie' was one of the June 1947 built examples from Swindon which until May 1960 was allocated to Newton Abbot but on this date in September 1960 was on the strength of Exeter St Davids shed so, presumably, the tank had hauled this train from Exeter. Like many of the locomotives which ended up at Woodhams scrapyard in Barry, this 2-6-2T went into preservation, just one of seven of the 4100-4179 batch alone which made it.

Further down the branch towards Kingswear we come across the junction station at Churston where a short branch line to Brixham diverged from the arm of the main branch (the bay used by the push-pull branch train was situated just out of frame to the left of the signal box). Seemingly working 'wrong line' Exeter based 'County' No.1023 COUNTY OF OXFORD has charge of this Kingswear-Bristol train in September 1960 and is stopping to pick-up intending passengers. The 4-6-0 is as usual in an atrocious external condition though mechanically it was still sound and would be for a couple of years yet. It was not condemned until March 1963 but it had been out-of-use at Shrewsbury shed since before the previous Christmas. Diesel hydraulic B-B Type 4 locomotives had already infiltrated this line and since August 1959 had been hauling the prestige *TORBAY EXPRESS* between Kingswear and Paddington and return. On the Plymouth line there was a daily total of eight Up express passenger workings hauled Type 4 diesel locomotives. Indeed the Brixham services were taken over by a two-car Derby-built d.m.u. for the 1961 season - 14XX 0-4-2T No.1456 had charge of the one coach train on this day. Nowadays of course this whole line is part of the Paignton & Dartmouth Steam Railway and is once again catering for the holiday crowds and tourists, Churston is virtually unchanged save for a few additions - long may it live.

Having doubled back and rejoined the main line to Plymouth at Aller junction, we have passed through Totnes and now come to Brent. Situated about midway between Newton Abbot and Plymouth, and inside the southern border of the Dartmoor National Park, Brent was the junction for the branch to Kingsbridge and was opened with the main line about 1848. Extensive reconstruction took place when the branch to Kingsbridge was constructed in the early 1890's, at the same time as the broad gauge was abolished. On a damp September day in 1960, 'Castle' No.5058 EARL OF CLANCARTY has just rounded the curve from the west and is bearing down on the station with a Penzance-Paddington express and is not about to either slow down or stop. The 4-6-0 is one of Laira's own and is immaculately turned-out for this important working. In September 1961, with the growing fleet of diesels working the main line trains, and with Authority trying its hardest to make the WR lines south of Bristol all diesel by 1962, the Earl moved on and found a home at Horton Road shed in Gloucester but the respite was only temporary. In January 1963 it was called into Swindon works for overhaul but was found to be in need of some expensive surgery. Condemned in March, it was cut up at Swindon, its birthplace, in April.

21

Flying through on the Down main at Brent that day is another 'Castle' No.4087 CARDIGAN CASTLE in charge of a Birmingham-Penzance express. This was a further example of Laira's finest and 83D managed to keep hold of this one until March 1963; no doubt failing diesel locomotives and the harsh 1962-63 winter kept it strategically placed until the worst was over. Its final shed was St Philips Marsh where it undertook six months work before being laid up, condemned and eventually sold off for scrap to a local yard. To the right of our picture is the Kingsbridge branch train with Newton Abbot based 45XX class 2-6-2T No.4561 working the branch passenger service. An engine shed was provided at Kingsbridge for the engine which would stay on the job for about a week at a time before being relieved by another of its kind. In latter years Nos.4555, 5558, 5564 and 5573 were all regular performers on this turn. Used for servicing the needs of travellers to the seaside resort at Salcombe, the Kingsbridge branch had three intermediate stations along its length but the whole lot closed at the end of the summer timetable in September 1963. The engine shed had closed two years previously when diesel units had replaced the steam workings. Not far behind the branch closure, Brent station closed in October 1964 and only the main line remains to remind us of a railway installation that is now long gone and, no doubt, will soon be forgotten.

Now we enter Plymouth (North Road) station, albeit on a Down goods train but nevertheless we have arrived. Heading this mixed bunch of vans, china clay wagons, and petrol tanks, is 5MT 'Grange' No.6873 CARADOC GRANGE, a Laira 4-6-0 which is in surprisingly poor external condition - perhaps mixed traffic engines did not warrant the cleaning given to the 'Castles'. The date is late August 1960 and big changes were afoot at North Road. The station itself had been undergoing reconstruction since 1956 and the end was now in sight with only the resignalling scheme and the new power box to be commissioned (the official 'opening' of the station did not take place until late March 1962). Note the new colour light signals on their gantries ready and waiting for the big switch-on. We are looking east, towards Mutley Plain, where the double bore tunnel which took the railway beneath the district, became a big problem which was never resolved by the railway authorities and for more than a century was a bottle-neck for traffic. Another aspect of the modern era being thrust upon the Region was the diesel multiple unit and one of them can be seen lurking in the siding behind the passing china clay wagons.

23

Monday 29th August 1960 - washing day for many and especially for the hardy souls who live back-to-back with the railway here at North Road. The crew of 'Modified Hall' No.6988 SWITHLAND HALL seem oblivious to the textiles blowing in the wind but I should imagine some Instruction existed somewhere, and which was issued aeons ago, pointing out the evils of producing excessive smoke and upsetting the public whilst tending to the needs of the engine at this location. Such complaints were a daily, if not hourly, occurrence at some places. It was a nation-wide problem for the railway. The paper work involved in sorting out the irate members of the public, not to mention the footplate crews, must have taken up a fair amount of time. There were many who were glad to see the back of steam - and that's before you mention the public. This rather smart looking 4-6-0 was a recent addition to Laira's stud although it had spent much of the fifties at 83D before transferring to Bristol for a year in 1959. The notice next to the tender was warning crews to beware that locomotives using the turntable could use wrong line working on return!

24

BR-built 'Modified Hall' No.7921 EDSTONE HALL, of September 1950 vintage, rolls into Plymouth (North Road) from Millbay carriage sidings with the empty stock of an afternoon Plymouth-Newton Abbot 'local'.. The date is September 1960 and the ten year old 4-6-0 appears to be in ex works condition but the truth is that Laira shed have kept up its ex Swindon appearance from its previous 'shopping'.. From new this engine was allocated to Chester (WR) shed but moved to Shrewsbury in August 1958. The following June it transferred to Plymouth but shortly after this picture was captured it went to Old Oak Common.

Onwards into Cornwall now and as soon as we cross the Tamar we arrive at Saltash station where time has gone backwards and we are now in July 1956. Our motive power from Plymouth was push-pull fitted 0-6-0PT No.6406 from Laira depot, a regular engine on the North Road-Saltash 'local'. The six-coupled tank was one of six 64XX allocated to the Plymouth shed during the post-war years for duties such as this. They were afforded fully lined green livery and kept in a reasonable external condition with overhauls carried out at Newton Abbot shops. The train is standing at the Down platform but its return to Plymouth over the Up main line will not require any crossing of points within the precincts of Saltash station as the single line crossing the Royal Albert bridge will automatically put it on the right track once it has traversed Brunel's masterpiece.

By the time we get to Liskeard (Change here for the Looe branch.) our time machine is playing tricks on us and has taken us forward to August 1960 once again. However, there is still plenty of steam around and our first meeting is with mixed traffic 'Grange' No.6854 ROUNDHILL GRANGE which is thundering through the station with an Up milk train bound for Kensington. This train, comprising six six-wheel tanks, a churn van and a flat car with a road trailer tank, will pickup further vehicles before it gets to Taunton whereby it will have doubled in length and weight. This train had originated at Penzance from where it departed at midday. It would be in London well before midnight, even with all the picking up en route. It was preceded from Penzance by a similar morning service. Milk trains were a great source of revenue for the railways, the Western Region especially, and they were run to a tight and regular schedule every day including Sundays. That traffic no longer exists, yet another rail-borne product now given over to road transportation. No.6854 was a relative newcomer to this part of the Region having been at Oxford for five years prior to its transfer to Laira in February 1960. Note the mail bags on the platform trolley waiting for an Up service for onward distribution.

Bodmin Road station was the main line connection of the branch to Bodmin General and the Southern Region branch line to Wadebridge. We shall venture along that branch later, once we have finished off our visit to the former Great Western lines in Cornwall, it will in fact be our access to the north Cornwall lines of the former L&SWR. However, in September 1960 the branch train from here to Wadebridge was in the charge of 45XX small Prairie No.4565, which had been supplied by St Blazey shed for this service. The main line platforms were on the other side of the stairway. The notices beneath the canopy on the far wall make interesting reading with daily fares to destinations near and not so far reading as follows: Looe - 2/9d; St Ives 7/9d; Penzance 8/9d; Falmouth 6/9d; Hayle 6/9d; Truro 4/9d. I'm not going to convert into new pence but three return journeys to Falmouth for a pound seems reasonable. Bodmin Road is now renamed Bodmin Parkway and is still in business whilst General station was closed in 1967.

St Blazey shed had a number of the smaller Prairie 2-6-2Ts allocated to work the local branches. This is No.5502, a Modified 45XX, running round its train at Bodmin Road station prior to working back to Wadebridge in July 1956. Besides six of the 55XX series engines, the small open roundhouse at 83E also had three times that number of the 45XX series engines allocated during much of the BR era. No.5502 was withdrawn in July 1958 at Swindon works but instead of being broken up there, as was the usual procedure up to that period, the little tank was sold for scrap to a private contractor - Cashmores at Newport. It was one of the first ex Great Western engines to be sold for scrap by British Railways and was hauled to South Wales in April 1959. Note the substantial water gantry spanning the tracks so that branch engines could top up whilst in the platform. Being summertime, the brazier is tucked away at the end of the platform, its presence adjacent to the gantry will not be required for some months yet.

29

Heading further west now (although the line thus far from Bodmin Road has gone mainly in a southerly direction), we reach Lostwithiel just in time to cross to the Up platform and photograph the following Paddington-Penzance express hauled by 'County' No.1023 COUNTY OF OXFORD. We have travelled forward in time once again to August 1960 and note the growing number of diesel era paraphernalia cropping up about the place - the 9 car stop sign, at the north end of this platform, being one of them. Note also the super elevation of the Up and Down tracks, not usually so visible but with the visual aids of the speeding train and the sleepered timber crossing between the platforms especially, it is readily discernible. Lostwithiel station was opened in 1859 but at some period was rebuilt by the GWR. Like many of the stations on this main line it is still open today. The 4-6-0 was an Exeter engine at this time having transferred from Penzance eleven months previously. It moved to Swindon in march 1961 and then to Shrewsbury for its last two years of operational life. Withdrawn in March 1963, after being stored for four months, it was sent to Swindon works in April 1963 and broken up, one of only three of the class scrapped there.

Onwards now to Par, passing the branch line to Fowey en route. Par (Change for Newquay) was one of the more interesting junctions on this line, the china clay traffic making it more so. We have arrived on this Plymouth-Truro train hauled by a rather clean looking Collett 'Grange' No.6802 BAMPTON GRANGE of Laira shed. Of course, it is July 1956 once again so things appear to be somewhat cleaner and carriage sets have a little bit more of the 'ancient' about them. From here the branch line to Newquay, and numerous, short, goods branches, leaves the main line and strikes out north to meet the Fowey to St Blazey line at the latter place. The platform on which the photographer is standing was double faced, the north face, out of sight behind the signal box, served the branch passenger services. Most of the main line expresses stopped here (and still do, Cornwall being peculiar in that 'express' passenger trains stop at about six or seven of the intermediate stations between Penzance and Plymouth - probably more than any other county).

Modified 45XX No.5538 departs from Par with a three-coach branch train to Newquay in August 1960. This was probably the last summer season when rail traffic to Newquay had the monopoly for moving holidaymakers from the junction here to the coast. Afterwards, the motor car started to take its toll and then foreign holidays bit into the whole of the UK holiday market. Newquay would never recover those halcyon days of post-war summers but whilst we have the memories and the photographic delights we can look back with great big dollops of nostalgia and enjoy the view. Is it me or does the telegraph pole have a resemblance to a strand of DNA? You certainly do not see many like that on model railway layouts. As mentioned, it is now 1960 and the 2-6-2T is hardly identifiable, at least by number but it was a newcomer to this part of the Region having spent the previous ten years at Horton Road Gloucester. It had transferred to Truro during the previous January but was on loan to St Blazey until the end of the summer timetable. The goods shed on the left is long gone but Par station is still as important as ever, at least for the main line, whilst the branch to Newquay is just about holding its own, helped no doubt by the china clay traffic generated at Goonbarrow junction. However, having stated that, the five intermediate stations: Luxulyan, Bugle, Roche, St.Columb Road, and Quintrel Downs, which were situated along its length in 1960 and forty-eight years later, still operational, so it can't be that bad.

A Newquay bound train leaves Par on a warm and sunny evening in July 1956. The motive power is a large Prairie, No.4167, the only one of its class to work in Cornwall during the British Railways era. Allocated to St Blazey at this time, it had spent time at Truro depot prior to its November 1954 transfer to St Blazey. The preference for the small wheeled Prairie tank in this part of the Region makes one wonder why this singleton was here for so long, however, the twenty-one mile branch to Newquay would have given it a decent run as the line was not as twisting as many other Cornish branch lines. The 41XX left Cornwall in September 1960 for Worcester, and more suited work perhaps. 33

An evening Plymouth-Truro local train departs Par in July 1956 with Laira 'Hall' No.6978 HAROLDSTONE HALL in charge. The spur in the foreground allowed access from the Up main into the branch side of the island platform. That line too is still in situ today and allows great flexibility at this junction station. No.6978 moved away from Cornwall during the following January and spent the next eight years working out of Old Oak Common shed. It ended its career working goods traffic from Severn Tunnel Junction and then latterly from Ebbw Junction shed in Newport. After withdrawal in July 1965, it was sold to a scrapyard in Swansea.

Back to August 1960 and things are beginning to squeak. We have travelled a further nineteen miles to one of Cornwall's larger towns - Truro - where the driver of No.6837 FORTHAMPTON GRANGE applies a drop of oil to the motion of the 4-6-0 before departure to Penzance with this local from Plymouth. From here the 'Grange' will keep to the main line whilst the twelve mile long branch to Falmouth cuts off at Penwithers junction and heads due south. The bay for the Falmouth trains is on the right, behind the engine. In 1960 the branch had three intermediate stations or rather two stations and a platform at Penmere; nowadays all three are halts. Crossing the Truro station site and dominating this end to some degree, is a girder footbridge which led from Station Road and carried a right-of-way enabling the public not just to cross over the station and main line but also across the throat of the goods yard and engine shed - it must have been a popular location for local enthusiasts.

Later that evening, a reasonably turned out 'Hall' No.4920 DUMBLETON HALL worked an Up freight onto the through goods lines on the north side of the station, passing the shed outlet road in the process. The 4-6-0 was allocated to Newton abbot at this time but it would end up at Oxford in November 1965, a transfer which probably saved its bacon as it was purchased by Woodham's and, well the rest is ......

Truro engine shed (BR code 83F) was situated in a slight depression on the north side of the main line, west of the station. Besides the three road shed building, yard and coal stage, the depot had an overgirder turntable which was typically GWR with its shallow pit. Part of the turntable can be seen in this pleasing view from August 1960, looking up towards the main line west of the station. 2-6-2T No.5552 is out of service and appears to be awaiting a trip to works for overhaul. It was however, withdrawn in October and was hauled to Barry for scrapping at Woodham's but that did not happen and after more than twenty years lying derelict it was purchased for preservation and the rest... It might appear to some readers that we have chosen pictures to use in this album which feature locomotives that are now preserved. I can assure them that this is not the case. What is apparent is the large number of GWR engines which made it into preservation. 37

Next stop Chacewater - 285 miles from London - still August 1960. This delightful scene shows the island platform on the Up side with a train from the Newquay branch just arriving behind 2-6-2T No.5564, a newcomer to the St Blazey strength. The elevated position of the station afforded commanding views across the countryside but closure in October 1964 rendered such views unobtainable except from passing trains. This platform was swept away after closure but the Down platform is apparently still visible though inaccessible. This was yet another junction station where decisions had to be made - stick to the main line or take the branch to Newquay. If the latter was chosen in 1960 there would be ten stops for the stations and halts over this section of line, a nice way to spend a pleasant afternoon. After 4th February 1963 it would have been impossible to have taken the train to Newquay from here because the branch was closed and allowed to disappear into memories. Note the GWR motif adorning the platform seat supports, the neat flowerbed and the 305 milepost, the original mileage from London over the Great Way Round route through Bristol! The Prairie tank had quite an interesting BR career having time at Bristol Bath Road, Swindon, Aberbeeg, Pontypool Road, Shrewsbury, St Blazey, Newton Abbot, Plymouth Laira, and finally Southall where, in December 1964 it was condemned. It had the dubious distinction of being one of the few BR steam locomotives to have been cut up in a London scrap yard.

If you were catching a Paddington bound train in July 1956 from Gwinear Road, this is what you would have encountered - hopefully. The Penzance based 5MT No.6826 NANNERTH GRANGE, was nicely turned out and already has a fair load behind it - the length of the train helps us appreciate the gradient here, even with the smoke haze. The train has a nice assortment of stock, all of it GWR in origin and the expectant passengers are lined up ready to board for their sedate but picturesque passage through Cornwall. On the way through the Duchy they would pass no less than thirteen branch lines and stop at nearly as many stations or so it would seem. Nowadays only six branch lines are encountered but the station stops are just as numerous. Gwinear Road was one of the junction stations mentioned forming the junction with the branch to Helston eight miles to the south. The photographer is standing on the Down platform which was actually an island platform with the Helston trains using the out platform face. The usual motive power for the branch trains was a 45XX 2-6-2T which was supplied by Penzance depot but which worked the branch for a week, staying overnight in a small stone built shed at Helston. The shed dated from 1887 and closed in 1963 when the last of the goods traffic ceased on the branch. Passenger facilities had been abolished during 1962. Gwinear Road had no place or purpose once the branch line had gone and it closed in October 1964.

39

In a view very similar to the previous one but taken four years later, an eight-coach Penzance to Truro train slows for the stop at Gwinear Road. No sign of any intending passengers for this one - perhaps they were getting in practice for the station closure four years hence. Another 5MT, No.6823 OAKLEY GRANGE is the motive power, this time one of the Truro batch.

We get to our last junction station, just a few miles down the line at St Erth where, in July 1956, 'Castle' No.4099 KILGERRAN CASTLE has charge of a five-coach Penzance-Plymouth local. The 7P 4-6-0 was a Penzance engine on this date, having transferred from Newton Abbot in the Spring of 1955. It transferred again in October 1957 to Landore depot but No.4095 HARLECH CASTLE arrived at Penzance from Swansea in exchange. Getting underway, the 'Castle' is signalled for the main line whilst the other signal controlled the branch line to St Ives. One of the shortest of the Cornish branches, it is still operational although the ten-coach portions of the *CORNISH RIVIERA* no longer traverse its metals as in days of old.

It is now August 1960 and seen running into St Erth with a short freight is that rarest of beasts - the Cornish 'Manor'. This is No.7806 COCKINGTON MANOR. Actually nearly a third of the class was allocated to depots in Devon and Cornwall throughout most of the period from 1951 to 1960 but no more than three of those were resident in Cornwall at any one time and, for most of that period only St Blazey shed had one to hand. When this photograph was captured No.7806 had been 'in county' for nearly a year at St Blazey and was soon about to transfer away to the West Midlands. This was not the first time this engine had been shedded in the Duchy as it had transferred to Penzance on September 1950 after ten years at Banbury. In December of that year it went to St Blazey for twelve months after which it went east to Newton Abbot for nearly four years. Truro had it briefly from July to October 1955 after which it moved to west Wales to work the Cambrian lines for a four year stint. Although nine of the class have been preserved, this engine was not one of them. It was in the wrong place where easy access by a Midlands scrap metal merchant saw it, secured for a song, and then cut up at Great Bridge in February 1965. The line leading off to the left of the engine is the start of the branch to St Ives which opened in June 1877.

Yes it is still August 1960 and no your eyes are not deceiving you - it is a clean 'County' and, a Bristol Bath Road one at that. This is No.1028 **COUNTY OF WARWICK** in charge of *THE CORNISHMAN* which it will work as far as Bristol (Temple Meads) where an ex LMS 'Jubilee' will take over. Note the St Erth railwaymen swapping banter with the driver as the 4-6-0 slowly gets underway. Situated 300 miles from London by the 'new' route, the station here opened in March 1852 and was apparently named St Ives Road until the opening of the branch when it was renamed. Serving a local population of about 2,000, the settlement of St Erth was nearly a mile away but residential sprawl has crept closer since WW2. A branch train waits in the bay, as still happens today.

Finally we arrive in Penzance on a damp afternoon in August 1960 but we are just in time to capture on film this incoming service from Truro headed by local boy No.6824 ASHLEY GRANGE. Penzance shed was well-off with these small-wheeled mixed traffic engines which were ideal locomotives for the main line route through Cornwall and beyond. This view, looking north along the main line towards Long Rock and Marazion, shows, in the hazy distance, the engine shed. The line of carriages in the middle distance mark the site of an earlier engine shed which closed in 1914 when the replacement at Long Rock was opened. So, we have reached the western most point of our journey into Cornwall having travelled along the southern edge of the county, the way of the GWR. We have now to retrace our steps to Bodmin General so that we will gain access to the northern parts of the county where the London & South Western Railway made

their mark.

Not only are we going backwards from whence we came now, we are going back in time once more and meet up with 'County' No.1028 at Penzance engine shed a few hours before it took up its working on *THE CORNISHMAN*. As can be seen the cleaners at Penzance depot had made a reasonable job of cleaning the 4-6-0 but ladders must have been at a premium or they were all short-ars..... Anyway, enough criticism, it looks a damn sight better now than what it did on arrival the previous day. Of course we tend to forget that recruiting footplate staff in the late fifties and early sixties was becoming a difficult job in itself. Other new, lighter and cleaner industries were taking school leavers away from the traditional forms of employment such as the railway. Whatever personnel was attracted to the footplate had to be kept at all costs, so it made sense to get them shovelling coal into a firebox and learning the ropes of firing and tending to a steam locomotive out on the road. Better than having them stuck in a fume filled shed with a paraffin rag rubbing off a thick, greasy mess which contaminated everything. Ironically, at the same time, the motive power authorities were 'shedding' jobs and closing depots as the new diesel units came into traffic, so it was really a no-win situation for the steam locomotive. In the West Country area of the Western Region dieselisation was very quickly taken up, and steam was virtually eliminated by the end of 1962. However, in August 1960 Penzance does not appear to have any diesels about the shed. Behind No.1028 is a 'Manor' - could it be No.6?

It is still August 1960 and we are still 'on shed' at 83G. The turntable holds another 'Grange' - the life and soul of Penzance depot during the post-war years. No.6854 was named ROUNDHILL GRANGE and was at this time a Laira engine, although during November it would transfer to Penzance for the winter season - sort of holiday really at 83G - before moving east again but only down the road to Truro. Resident No.6860 ABERPORTH GRANGE looks on from the side knowing that it will soon be leaving Penzance for Llanelly depot and might not return to this place. In the event it didn't, at least not by transfer. It was reallocated to Plymouth during the following summer so presumably would have worked in during its time there. Both engines ended up as scrap but were not withdrawn until 1965, September and February respectively.

I know, yet another 'Grange' not only that but we met this dirty specimen in Plymouth some pages back. It was that same goods train which brought the 5MT here on this glorious August morning. Anyway, the shed is fairly quiet and there is ample space to look around. As already mentioned, this depot was opened in 1914 and its layout was such that future expansion would easily have been accommodated. The four road running shed was adequate right to the end however. Behind the smokebox of the 4-6-0 can be seen the entrance to the repair shop which enabled Penzance to be fairly self sufficient regarding most minor repairs. Newton Abbot shed, the concentration depot 83A in the BR scheme was some distance away even as the crow flies so add the twists and turns of the main line and you have a heck of a distance to tow a dead engine. Besides 83A had the nearby works or factory too. So, it made sense to have some facilities down here. This depot closed in September 1962, the Monday the 10th was the official day when Western Region steam was effectively banned west of Saltash. 47

For our last look at Penzance steam power we go back in time to the east end of the shed yard in July 1956. We have a different class to look at now, a 'Modified Hall', No.7925 WESTOL HALL, a British Railways built example which was less than six years old when captured on film by Don Beecroft. This 5MT had been at Penzance since being put into traffic in November 1950 and it has certainly been looked after judging by its external appearance. It is probably making its way off shed to back down to the station to take on an eastbound working so it might be a good idea to hitch a ride as far as Bodmin Road. Behind is a more senior 'Hall' No.5926 GROTRIAN HALL. Farewell Penzance.

There are at least four members of station staff in this view of Bodmin (General) in August 1960, two with their caps flicked to one side in that nonchalant fashion of the period. The train is the Bodmin (Road) to Wadebridge where the old enemy is once again encountered. For such a small town, Bodmin (population 5526 in 1935) was well blessed with two railway stations, one entering from the north via the Southern Region [LSWR] route to Bodmin (North) and the other from the south via the Western Region [GWR] route to Bodmin (General). Both places had full goods facilities with warehousing, craneage and private sidings. Of course that kind of repetitive extravagance could not last - it was just what Dr. Beeching was looking for - but in the summer of 1960 everything carried on as normal as here; SR trains ran from Wadebridge to Bodmin (North) whilst WR trains trod the same path as far as Boscarne junction then used Bodmin (General) station. Admitted, the SR had the Wenford Bridge branch to worry about but that was a dying concern by now. Ironically, one of the two SR O2 class engines which worked the Bodmin passenger services was taken off that job in 1960 (condemned) and the work was then given to WR Pannier tanks drafted in to Wadebridge shed for the purpose - the WR were making their mark on the Southern lines before they made their mark! The two Bodmin stations closed in January 1967 by which time the whole county was chocolate and cream, the out-of-town establishment on the main line and known as Bodmin Road was kept open being renamed Parkway in 1983 - the GWR had won that one. 49

Yes it is 2-6-2T No.4552 again, with the same train (rolling stock) as in the previous illustration (but some days later) and now it is in Southern Region territory, at Wadebridge station - concrete land, September 1960. Wadebridge was one of those stations that had everything a model railway would need - island platform and connecting footbridge (in concrete) with the main platform, ticket office and entrance hall, waiting rooms, etc., goods yard (smallish) with shed (with concrete extension), cattle dock (concrete), coal merchants, engine shed (small) with turntable and, eventually, a smart coaling shed. There was a river bordering two sides of the layout, with bridges and attendant wharves. The London & South Western Railway got to Wadebridge in 1895 by a somewhat torturous 88-mile route from Exeter via Okehampton, Halwill and Launceston. Much of the line was single with passing loops at stations. Further LSWR expansion into north Devon too brought with it some duplication of routes but it did keep the GWR out of a wide ranging expanse of Devon and Cornwall. The various branches demanded dedicated motive power and rolling stock which came together at strategic junction stations to form one train (the *ATLANTIC COAST EXPRESS* comes to mind but there were others). From Wadebridge the line went even further west to Padstow, another five and a half miles, which was essentially the most westerly place on the LSWR - Southern Railway - SReg.

Wadebridge station July 1956 with 2-6-2T No.5502 running round its train (on platform No.3) ready to work back to Bodmin Road. We saw this St Blazey based engine earlier at Bodmin Road just as it was about to work this particular service. At this time the two Regions between them had five sets of carriages plying between Bodmin Road, Bodmin (General and North), Wadebridge and Padstow everyday, the Western Region engines supplied by St Blazey with Wadebridge supplying the Adams O2 tanks. It took one hour exactly to travel from Bodmin Road to Padstow, with all the relevant stops and the necessary reversing. Note how clean the whole place appears to be, even the engine shed roof, in the background, has a certain cleanliness about it.

Now this is what we came to see at Wadebridge. No.30587 was one of the trio of Beattie 2-4-0 well tanks which had been at Wadebridge since time began, or so it seemed. Their history on the Wenford Bridge line has been well chronicled and on this day in July 1956 one of them was away working that duty, one might have been on shed but could have been away at Eastleigh works, leaving this one to shunt the station and goods yard. The fireman, or was it the driver, anyway they were part of Wadebridge shed No.5 Link, appear to be having an easy time of it, the swinging leg hanging out over the cab side sheet indicating a moment of daydreaming perhaps. The wooden engine shed, complete with glass (they must have employed a full-time window cleaner) still in the window frames, appears to be in very good condition. The Beattie tanks officially finished work on the Wenford job on Monday 13th August 1962, with the small-wheeled WR Pannier '1366' class tanks taking over on the following day.

Unrebuilt 'Battle of Britain' No.34063 229 SQUADRON, of Exmouth Junction, enters Wadebridge from Halwill with a train for Padstow in September 1960. Padstow was the only station around which had a turntable long enough to turn the Pacifics. There was no engine shed but at least the turntable was big enough so every Pacific which arrived at Wadebridge had to make the short though winding trip along the bank of the Camel estuary. Padstow was not reached by the LSWR until March 1899, quite late considering the Bodmin & Wadebridge Railway had been on the doorstep since 1834 albeit connected to nowhere. The filthy Pacific was to remain in this condition i.e. unrebuilt, and filthy probably, until withdrawal in August 1965. By then it would have transferred a couple of times, firstly to Brighton in May 1963 then to Salisbury four months later.

Having worked in from Exeter earlier in the day, Exmouth Junction T9 No.30708, by now serviced, makes its way from the turntable past Wadebridge shed yard, ready to work back home on the mid afternoon train to Exeter (Central) in July 1956. The T9 still has its eight-wheel tender and would keep it to withdrawal even though many of the class had by now been coupled to six-wheel types. Long standing passenger motive power on the North Cornwall line and daily visitors to Wadebridge, the T9 class would continue on such jobs until condemnations whittled their numbers down to the final two which left Exmouth Junction shed for scrap in July 1961. No.30708 was withdrawn just eighteen months after this picture was captured and was taken to Eastleigh for breaking up. Note that WR 2-6-2T No.5502 has now coupled up to its Bodmin Road bound train on the island platform; this would be the 3-24 p.m. departure.

O2 class 0-4-4T No.30200 was one of two of its kind allocated to Wadebridge during BR days - No.30203 was the other. Of course the O2 class had been at the depot since 1900 and probably before, to work the Bodmin (North) to Padstow passenger service. In 1933 Nos.216 and 221 were resident. In September 1951 No.30192 joined the regular duo from Exmouth Junction but it then transferred to Plymouth Friary some eighteen months later. When No.30203 was withdrawn in December 1955, Friary shed sent No.30236 to replace it. By July 1956, when this picture was taken in the shed yard, the two O2 class on the Wadebridge strength was still being maintained and would remain that way until January 1960 when No.30236 was condemned at Eastleigh works. No.30200 was on its own now but the small-wheeled WR 0-6-0PT started to arrive, not only to replace the withdrawn O2 but also to oust the remaining Adams engine which was put into store at Wadebridge. No.30200 left the North Cornwall line in March 1961 for Eastleigh shed but suitable work could not be found for it there so it went to Friary shed in April 1962 to take the place of the last surviving O2 at that place, No.30193 which was promptly withdrawn on arrival at Eastleigh works. By the end of summer 1962 the little 0-4-4T left Plymouth for Eastleigh works and was cut up on arrival. Now, with our visit completed, we leave Wadebridge and travel along the North Cornwall line to venture deeper into SR territory to Halwill Junction.

Going forward in time once again to August 1960, we arrive at Halwill Junction to meet unrebuilt 'Battle of Britain' No.34072 257 SQUADRON which is just leaving with a three-coach train for Padstow. Halwill Junction became an important station in July 1886 when the line to Launceston was brought into use. The station was opened in January 1879 by the Devon & Cornwall Railway and was then named Halwill & Beaworthy, the present name was bestowed in March 1887 but the nameboards apparently remained unchanged. Although a turntable was installed on the west side of the goods yard, no engine shed was erected. In 1925 the line from Torrington reached Halwill which meant that Barnstaple was also linked via that route but little use was made of the link other than to serve the intermediate stations. Halwill station had contradictory nameboards, the main Up and Down platform nameboards proclaimed HALWILL FOR BEAWORTHY with the added JUNCTION FOR BUDE, NORTH CORNWALL & TORRINGTON LINES beneath. The Torrington platform nameboard announced simply HALWILL JUNCTION. As mentioned previously, the Exmouth Junction based Bullied Pacifics were, at this time in 1960, a woebegone bunch regarding cleanliness, their huge streamlined sideplating not helping matters any by advertising the accumulated filth. However, much later, around 1962, a new regime must have swept through 'The Junction' because the Pacifics suddenly appeared clean, as though a cleaning gang had been hired at 72A. No.34072's clean-up would take place somewhat sooner, during the following January, but only because it had to visit Eastleigh for an Intermediate overhaul.

Right behind us, from the Padstow direction, came N class 2-6-0 No.31836 an Up goods which included loaded cattle trucks. This mogul was one of the Woolwich Arsenal made engines dating from 1924 which was put together at Ashford works by the Southern and went on to serve the railways for more than forty years in most cases. This long standing member of the Exmouth Junction batch (the depot had twenty-one allocated in 1960) was in the usual 72A livery and some wag has taken advantage of the grime to expose certain numbers with connotations of bad luck - I am not aware of any such luck befalling the 2-6-0 then or at any other time leading up to its withdrawal in December 1963 at Exmouth Junction shed.

A little later on, when the late afternoon sun came out, another N, No.31842 (also Exmouth Junction based) came charging off the Bude branch with a similarly loaded goods train. The gradient was now in the favour of the train but within a mile it will encounter the mainly 1 in 78 uphill challenge to milepost 205 some five miles distant.

More sedately and with a little less weight behind, N class No.31843 sets off from Halwill with this Bude train in August 1960. The Torrington line platform, vacant just now, can be seen immediately behind the last carriage of this formation. The three routes radiating north-westward from Halwill run side by side just here, the nearest being the Padstow line, Bude, centre and Torrington and Barnstaple far left. By 1963 these Moguls would start giving way to BR Standard Class 4 2-6-4T engines on these services, Exmouth Junction getting a dozen of them allocated in June 1962. In the summer of 1964 they had virtually monopolised the lines west of Okehampton but the Light Pacifics and the N's were still in evidence. At the end of the summer timetable 1964 it did not matter what type of steam locomotive was in vogue or how old it was. Services over the former LSWR lines were cut back severely, the Beeching axe was falling and what services did remain were taken over by diesel units. The end was in sight for steam and eventually places like Halwill and all stations beyond.

Sticking with the late afternoon traffic for the moment, we see T9 No.30715 calling at Halwill with a train off the Bude line. The 4-4-0 was to be amongst the handful of its class which managed to work until early summer 1961. No.30715 entered Eastleigh works in June 1961, was condemned in July and cut up in August, their like never again to be seen on these lines. In the Down platform an Engineers motorised trolley makes for refuge onto the Bude line before the next main line service comes breathing down its neck. Once these two 'trains' have gone, quiet will descend once again on Halwill until the next arrivals materialise from the Atlantic coast or Exeter.

Ivatt Cl.2 No.41295 stands at the Torrington line platform at Halwill Junction, in August 1960, with the single coach which will make up the early evening service to Torrington. All that remains is for the engine to propel the carriage further up the line, run round and push it back to the platform for the 6-30 p.m. departure. For these duties the 2-6-2T was allocated to Barnstaple Junction depot, along with Nos.41294, 41297 and 41298. No.41295 would transfer to Plymouth Friary in August 1961 but the other three would stay on at Barnstaple until early 1963 when diesel railcars took over most of the services they ran from there.

Earlier in the afternoon at Halwill Junction on that August day in 1960, our old friend 'BB' No.34063 229 SQUADRON was waiting in the Down bay for the arrival of the Bude train from Exeter, ex Waterloo, which had a portion for Padstow. It was the latter portion which interested the Pacific and after working down to the coast it will retire for the night to Wadebridge shed to be serviced and put to bed ready for the early morning passenger train to Okehampton and Exeter after taking a goods to Padstow, turning and preparing the carriage set for the run over the North Cornwall line.

Signalled for the Launceston line, No.34063 departs Halwill with its lightweight load for Padstow in August 1960. It is easy, with hindsight, to see that the economies of running the railways in this part of south-west England were never going to show a profit but with a nationalised industry, a strategic one at that, do profits have to be made? Is not the railway there for the good of all, for all sorts of reasons? Does a profitable section of the system subsidise a loss-making part? By 1960 it was becoming very evident to most people that British Railways was a gigantic drain on the country hence the appointment of dear old Dr.B to sort things out. Much of it he did sort out and the railways of Devon and Cornwall were hard it when the crunch came. Services such as this one bring to mind hammers and nuts, and it was not just a one-off event either. This same scenario was being enacted day in, day out, and all day for years and even decades in some cases. It was cut and dried. Nice whilst it lasted but it was not going to last forever. At some stations in this part of the country they were dealing with a couple of passengers a week! 'Oh! Mr Porter' was nearer to the bone than we would like to admit.

Travelling from Halwill to Okehampton now, we come across Meldon Quarry halt which served men working at the quarry who lived away from the place and the wives of men who lived nearby and who wanted to travel to Okehampton to shop. The date is August 1960 and the narrow platform seems hardly the place to be with a non-stopping train rushing by. Obviously only certain trains stopped here to pick up and set down so arrival of train and pedestrian could be easily arranged. Besides the resident Departmental locomotives, the quarry employed an Exmouth Junction engine on occasion and O2 No.30199 is helping out this summer which seems a strange choice for the work carried out. This was the last O2 to be scrapped, the deed taking place at Eastleigh in December 1963. None of the mainland O2 class made it to preservation but luckily one of the Isle of Wight 'namers' managed it to be the sole representative of an attractive and useful ancient class.

On now to Okehampton where we find T9 No.30313 simmering on the goods shed road in the yard on the south side of the station, waiting to take on a portion of an express to either Padstow or Bude. The train will probably arrive behind a 'BB' or 'WC' which would take on the other portion. The engine shed at Okehampton was situated east of the station on the Up side of the line. A long, single road structure, it was built of concrete blocks and came into use in 1920 replacing a timber shed which had been destroyed by fire. In 1943 a 70ft diameter turntable was installed, with Pacifics in mind, on the site of the 50ft turntable which had in 1895 replaced the original 42ft turntable. Up to six T9 class 4-4-0s were shedded here, all outstationed from Exmouth Junction. In the post-war summers as many as nine would temporarily 'be on the books'. Of course they could not all be accommodated under cover and there would be no need to have such cover because a large proportion would be out on the road or stabling at Bude, Plymouth or Wadebridge overnight. The shed closed in 1964, the diesels then used having no need for turntables, coaling and watering facilities or covered stabling. No.30313 was not long on this job and was condemned at Eastleigh the following summer, its demise complete by September. 65

We drop down to Bere Alston now, only a few miles from Plymouth but we are still in Southern territory. Our first encounter in August 1960 is with this Plymouth-Waterloo express headed by 'West Country' No.34107 BLANDFORD FORUM, another of the SR Pacifics which managed to keep its original air-smooth casing. The six-coach load is nothing to bother this engine, even the continuous and winding climb up to Okehampton will be taken in its stride but the stop there will add a few more carriages to the make-up. Bere Alston station was opened in June 1890 and for the first seven years was known as Beer Alston before the alteration was made to give the station its present name (next station down the line to Plymouth, Bere Ferrers went through the same process). In March 1908 the 9½ mile long Callington branch, seen on the right and heading off into the distance, was opened for traffic. With five intermediate stations and one halt along its course, the branch is, in part, still open today although only two of those stations exist, Calstock and Gunnislake; the last five miles to Callington being abandoned in November 1966. Those five miles remained operational longer than the 'WC' because the Exmouth Junction Pacific was condemned in September 1964 and by Christmas of that year was in little pieces in a South Wales scrapyard! Bere Alston seems to have survived thus far and is now part of the Plymouth commuter belt along with the branch just mentioned. Reversal of the diesel unit has to take place for access to the branch but that is a small price to pay for having a branchline meandering through the Tamar valley. Note the L&SWR notices at the bottom of each platform ramp. In immaculate condition, they state that 'Passengers must cross line by bridge' - short and sweet. The signal post appears to be one of those fabricated from old rails but is nevertheless well maintained. Something is 'pegged' on the Down line, I wonder what.

Light engine movement towards Plymouth in the shape of N class No.31853. The 2-6-0 was a recent arrival at Exmouth Junction shed from Bricklayers Arms and was destined to spend the rest of its operational life working in Devon and Cornwall. After being condemned in September 1964 it was stored at the former Great Western engine shed at Exeter before being purchased for scrap by a yard in Swansea. Note the two Engineers motorised trolley sheds on the Up side - one day somebody might write a book about these lesser known pieces if railway infrastructure and there occupants.

Plymouth Friary shed supplied the motive power for the Bere Alston-Callington passenger services. In August 1960 Adams O2 No.30225, one of only eight still operational on the mainland, was in charge of this afternoon working to Callington which has just departed from Bere Alston. The branch train could consist two passenger coaches as here, or a single coach with a couple of vans - a mixed train, depending on seasonal trends. Much of the goods workings were undertaken by Ivatt 2-6-2T and these little 0-4-4T usually kept themselves to the passenger workings until diesel power came along but the Ivatt's also worked the passenger services too. The Callington branch trains used the north face of the Down platform which had become an island for that purpose. The Up and Down platforms were linked by a footbridge which, since the twenties, had been a concrete structure.

In March 1953 Plymouth Friary shed took delivery of its first Ivatt Cl.2 tank engine, No.41315, which had transferred from Exmouth Junction. The 2-6-2T then started a relationship with the depot which was to last until the place closed in May 1963. By then three others of the same class had joined the Pathfinder - Nos.41316 in November 1956, 41302 in December 1956, and 41317 in June 1957. No.41314 made a brief appearance in November 1956, courtesy of Bricklayers Arms but it returned to London after only a few weeks. The main purpose of the Ivatt tanks transfer to Friary in 1956 was to take over from the fifty-years old Plymouth, Devonport & South Western Junction 0-6-2Ts, Nos.30757 EARL OF MOUNT EDGCUMBE and 30758 LORD ST.LEVAN. The latter two engines had been purchased in 1907 for the opening of the Callington branch and spent their nocturnal hours in a shed at the terminus once used for the East Cornwall Mineral Railway 3ft 6in. gauge motive power albeit in a rebuilt state. That shed closed in 1964 when steam was ousted from the branch. In this August 1960 view we have No.41316 heading the 'Pathfinder' across bridge No.1 (that serving the main line was No.683) as they come off the branch into Bere Alston with a mixed freight. The area between Bere Alston and Callington (Kellybray as it was known pre-PD&SWJR days) was once the copper mining capital of Britain, if not the world - much of the present world production not having been discovered then - but now that industry is long gone and only a few relics remain. Callington terminus was in fact situated in the village of Kellybray, the village of Callington being more than a mile distant to the south. At opening in 1908 the PD&SWJR named the station Callington Road but Road was dropped soon afterwards.

Our final look at Bere Alston, and south-west Devon, brings into focus the penultimate Bullied Light Pacific 'BB' No.34109, which also had the longest name, SIR TRAFFORD LEIGH-MALLORY. Soon to be rebuilt and effectively banned from all but this route west of Exeter, No.34109 is working the last five coaches, the Plymouth portion, of a Down express from Waterloo. The sweeping curve through this place will take it from a westerly heading to a southerly one for the last 9½ miles to Devonport (King's Road) station. In its rebuilt form the Pacific returned to Exmouth Junction shed in March 1961 and continued working this route but dieselisation saw its early demise in September 1964. We now journey back through Okehampton and on to Coleford junction where we gain access to the Barnstaple line. Our final visit is to Ilfracombe which is effectively due north from Bere Alston but we have to take the long-winded route just like the L&SWR did.

Our penultimate view takes us back in time once again to July 1956. We are at Ilfracombe on the north coast of Devon, looking at the one road engine shed and its attendant turntable created from a rocky hillside in 1928 by the Southern Railway. The original engine shed at this resort was situated on the east side of the terminal station but enlargement of the passenger facilities forced its removal to this site. Seen on the left of the picture is the main line to Barnstaple, quite steep at this point, being something like 1 in 37. Salisbury based 'West Country' No.34092 CITY OF WELLS slides past the shed after turning, and is making its way back to the station. Near the signal box can be seen an unidentifiable 'N' class 2-6-0, a type which held sway here before the coming of the Pacifics after the war. The 65ft turntable came before the shed but only just as the whole enterprise involved moving the engine facilities away from the station. Built from concrete blocks (what else), the shed structure might have been a prototype for the one-road diesel depots erected in the early years of dieselisation by the Eastern Region of British Railways - King's Cross, King's Lynn and others come to mind - a simple effective shelter with access either end. Closed in 1964, the derelict shed would look down on the main line which was at first singled, then in October 1970 closed completely. Ilfracombe was cut off from the railway network, another L&SWR line was but a memory. We take our leave now and head back to Exeter, thankful that Don Beecroft decided to stop off at Ilfracombe on his holiday travels in July 1956.

And so we come full circle - well nearly - ending our journey through Devon and Cornwall at Exeter's St Davids station. We entered from the south initially, off the Southern, and now we enter the station from the north just like the Western trains from London, although we have come from the exLSWR north Devon line. This is the north end of St Davids on a glorious September afternoon in 1960. As usual there was plenty happening here, comings and goings on the main line, shunting, banking or simply road and pedestrian traffic across the Red Cow manned level crossing. Standing on platform No.5, we can observe BR Standard Class 4 No.76018 entering with a short train which does not appear to be approaching the SR island platform (3 and 4 remember) but not was rigid anymore, it was all the same firm so to speak and only habits no stood in the way of progress or at least efficiency. Note the twelve-wheel vehicle behind the green SR carriage. The Horwich built 2-6-0 was on the Salisbury allocation at this time having come new to the Southern Region, at Eastleigh shed, in June 1953. Beyond the shadow of the signal box, Z class 0-8-0T No.30955, complete with, over the bufferbeam, a white disc denoting 'banking engine' waits in the background for further custom. By now all eight of the Z class engines were allocated to Exmouth Junction shed to work the mainly 1 in 37 bank between St Davids and Central stations although, as can be imagined, not all of them were employed for much of the time. No.30955 arrived at 'The Junction' in August 1958 from Ashford, the others followed from Salisbury and Templecombe. During November and December 1962 all eight of the 6F tanks were condemned, replaced for a short time by a trio of the W class 2-6-4T, Nos.31911, 31915 and 31916. However, with the Western Region taking control of the former SR lines in Devon in 1963, WR 0-6-0PTs took on the remaining banking duties. Finally, it is still possible to reach London from Exeter departing from either end of St Davids - old habits etc.!